50 Flavorful Asian-Inspired Stir-Frys

By: Kelly Johnson

Table of Contents

- Chicken and Broccoli Stir-Fry
- Beef and Bell Pepper Stir-Fry
- Shrimp and Snow Peas Stir-Fry
- Tofu and Vegetable Stir-Fry
- Cashew Chicken Stir-Fry
- Mongolian Beef Stir-Fry
- Spicy Szechuan Noodles with Vegetables
- Teriyaki Salmon Stir-Fry
- Garlic Ginger Shrimp and Asparagus
- Sweet and Sour Chicken Stir-Fry
- Vegetable Lo Mein Stir-Fry
- Thai Basil Beef Stir-Fry
- Black Bean Chicken Stir-Fry
- Sesame Tofu and Broccoli
- Orange Chicken Stir-Fry
- Hoisin Beef and Broccoli Stir-Fry
- Kung Pao Chicken Stir-Fry
- Garlic Snow Peas and Mushrooms
- Spicy Pork and Bok Choy Stir-Fry
- Sweet Chili Shrimp and Veggies
- Lemon Garlic Chicken Stir-Fry
- Pad Thai Vegetable Stir-Fry
- Korean Beef Bulgogi Stir-Fry
- Teriyaki Tofu and Vegetable Stir-Fry
- Thai Red Curry Chicken Stir-Fry
- Szechuan Eggplant Stir-Fry
- Honey Garlic Chicken and Broccoli
- Pineapple Chicken Stir-Fry
- Vegetable Fried Rice Stir-Fry
- Five-Spice Chicken and Vegetable Stir-Fry
- Cashew Shrimp Stir-Fry
- Spicy Garlic Tofu and Bell Peppers
- Cilantro Lime Chicken Stir-Fry
- Sweet and Sour Tofu Stir-Fry
- Spicy Asian Pork Stir-Fry

- Lemon Grass Chicken Stir-Fry
- Thai Peanut Chicken Stir-Fry
- Teriyaki Beef and Vegetable Stir-Fry
- Garlic Shrimp and Zucchini Stir-Fry
- Broccoli and Beef Stir-Fry with Oyster Sauce
- Miso Glazed Eggplant Stir-Fry
- Spicy Szechuan Chicken and Noodles
- Sesame Ginger Shrimp Stir-Fry
- Thai Coconut Chicken Stir-Fry
- Lemon Ginger Tofu Stir-Fry
- Egg Foo Young Stir-Fry
- Curry Vegetable Stir-Fry
- Stir-Fried Udon Noodles with Veggies
- Honey Soy Chicken and Veggie Stir-Fry
- Teriyaki Vegetable and Tofu Stir-Fry

Chicken and Broccoli Stir-Fry

Ingredients:

- 1 lb chicken breast, sliced
- 2 cups broccoli florets
- 2 cloves garlic, minced
- 1 tbsp ginger, minced
- 3 tbsp soy sauce
- 2 tbsp oyster sauce
- 1 tbsp sesame oil
- 1 tbsp vegetable oil
- Cooked rice for serving

Instructions:

1. **Heat Oil:** In a large skillet or wok, heat vegetable oil over medium-high heat.
2. **Cook Chicken:** Add sliced chicken and stir-fry for about 5-7 minutes until cooked through.
3. **Add Vegetables:** Add broccoli, garlic, and ginger; stir-fry for an additional 3-4 minutes until broccoli is tender but crisp.
4. **Add Sauce:** Stir in soy sauce, oyster sauce, and sesame oil. Cook for another minute.
5. **Serve:** Serve over cooked rice.

Beef and Bell Pepper Stir-Fry

Ingredients:

- 1 lb beef sirloin, thinly sliced
- 2 bell peppers (any color), sliced
- 2 cloves garlic, minced
- 1 tbsp ginger, minced
- 3 tbsp soy sauce
- 1 tbsp cornstarch
- 2 tbsp vegetable oil
- Cooked rice for serving

Instructions:

1. **Marinate Beef:** In a bowl, combine sliced beef with soy sauce and cornstarch; let marinate for 15 minutes.
2. **Heat Oil:** In a large skillet or wok, heat vegetable oil over medium-high heat.
3. **Cook Beef:** Add marinated beef and stir-fry for about 3-4 minutes until browned.
4. **Add Vegetables:** Add bell peppers, garlic, and ginger; stir-fry for an additional 3-4 minutes.
5. **Serve:** Serve over cooked rice.

Shrimp and Snow Peas Stir-Fry

Ingredients:

- 1 lb shrimp, peeled and deveined
- 2 cups snow peas
- 2 cloves garlic, minced
- 1 tbsp ginger, minced
- 3 tbsp soy sauce
- 1 tbsp sesame oil
- 1 tbsp vegetable oil
- Cooked rice for serving

Instructions:

1. **Heat Oil:** In a large skillet or wok, heat vegetable oil over medium-high heat.
2. **Cook Shrimp:** Add shrimp and stir-fry for about 2-3 minutes until pink and cooked through.
3. **Add Vegetables:** Add snow peas, garlic, and ginger; stir-fry for an additional 2-3 minutes.
4. **Add Sauce:** Stir in soy sauce and sesame oil. Cook for another minute.
5. **Serve:** Serve over cooked rice.

Tofu and Vegetable Stir-Fry

Ingredients:

- 14 oz firm tofu, pressed and cubed
- 2 cups mixed vegetables (carrots, bell peppers, broccoli)
- 2 cloves garlic, minced
- 1 tbsp ginger, minced
- 3 tbsp soy sauce
- 1 tbsp vegetable oil
- 1 tbsp sesame oil
- Cooked rice for serving

Instructions:

1. **Heat Oil:** In a large skillet or wok, heat vegetable oil over medium-high heat.
2. **Cook Tofu:** Add cubed tofu and stir-fry until golden brown, about 5-7 minutes.
3. **Add Vegetables:** Add mixed vegetables, garlic, and ginger; stir-fry for an additional 4-5 minutes until vegetables are tender.
4. **Add Sauce:** Stir in soy sauce and sesame oil. Cook for another minute.
5. **Serve:** Serve over cooked rice.

Cashew Chicken Stir-Fry

Ingredients:

- 1 lb chicken breast, diced
- 1 cup cashews
- 2 cups mixed vegetables (broccoli, bell peppers, carrots)
- 2 cloves garlic, minced
- 3 tbsp soy sauce
- 2 tbsp hoisin sauce
- 1 tbsp vegetable oil
- Cooked rice for serving

Instructions:

1. **Heat Oil:** In a large skillet or wok, heat vegetable oil over medium-high heat.
2. **Cook Chicken:** Add diced chicken and stir-fry for about 5-7 minutes until cooked through.
3. **Add Vegetables:** Add mixed vegetables and garlic; stir-fry for an additional 3-4 minutes.
4. **Add Sauce and Cashews:** Stir in soy sauce, hoisin sauce, and cashews. Cook for another minute.
5. **Serve:** Serve over cooked rice.

Mongolian Beef Stir-Fry

Ingredients:

- 1 lb flank steak, thinly sliced
- 1 cup green onions, chopped
- 2 cloves garlic, minced
- 1 tbsp ginger, minced
- 3 tbsp soy sauce
- 1 tbsp brown sugar
- 1 tbsp vegetable oil
- Cooked rice for serving

Instructions:

1. **Heat Oil:** In a large skillet or wok, heat vegetable oil over medium-high heat.
2. **Cook Beef:** Add sliced flank steak and stir-fry for about 3-4 minutes until browned.
3. **Add Onions and Garlic:** Add green onions, garlic, and ginger; stir-fry for an additional 2-3 minutes.
4. **Add Sauce:** Stir in soy sauce and brown sugar; cook for another minute.
5. **Serve:** Serve over cooked rice.

Spicy Szechuan Noodles with Vegetables

Ingredients:

- 8 oz noodles (spaghetti or rice noodles)
- 2 cups mixed vegetables (bell peppers, carrots, broccoli)
- 2 cloves garlic, minced
- 1 tbsp ginger, minced
- 3 tbsp Szechuan sauce
- 1 tbsp vegetable oil
- Sesame seeds for garnish

Instructions:

1. **Cook Noodles:** Cook noodles according to package instructions; drain and set aside.
2. **Heat Oil:** In a large skillet or wok, heat vegetable oil over medium-high heat.
3. **Add Vegetables:** Add mixed vegetables, garlic, and ginger; stir-fry for about 4-5 minutes.
4. **Combine Noodles:** Add cooked noodles and Szechuan sauce; stir-fry for another 2-3 minutes.
5. **Serve:** Garnish with sesame seeds and serve.

Teriyaki Salmon Stir-Fry

Ingredients:

- 1 lb salmon fillets, cubed
- 2 cups mixed vegetables (broccoli, bell peppers, snap peas)
- 2 cloves garlic, minced
- 1 tbsp ginger, minced
- 3 tbsp teriyaki sauce
- 1 tbsp vegetable oil
- Cooked rice for serving

Instructions:

1. **Heat Oil:** In a large skillet or wok, heat vegetable oil over medium-high heat.
2. **Cook Salmon:** Add cubed salmon and stir-fry for about 4-5 minutes until cooked through.
3. **Add Vegetables:** Add mixed vegetables, garlic, and ginger; stir-fry for an additional 3-4 minutes.
4. **Add Sauce:** Stir in teriyaki sauce and cook for another minute.
5. **Serve:** Serve over cooked rice.

Enjoy your delicious stir-fry meals!

Garlic Ginger Shrimp and Asparagus

Ingredients:

- 1 lb shrimp, peeled and deveined
- 1 lb asparagus, trimmed and cut into 2-inch pieces
- 3 cloves garlic, minced
- 1 tbsp ginger, minced
- 3 tbsp soy sauce
- 1 tbsp sesame oil
- 1 tbsp vegetable oil
- Cooked rice for serving

Instructions:

1. **Heat Oil:** In a large skillet or wok, heat vegetable oil over medium-high heat.
2. **Cook Shrimp:** Add shrimp and stir-fry for about 2-3 minutes until pink and cooked through.
3. **Add Asparagus:** Add asparagus, garlic, and ginger; stir-fry for an additional 3-4 minutes until asparagus is tender-crisp.
4. **Add Sauce:** Stir in soy sauce and sesame oil; cook for another minute.
5. **Serve:** Serve over cooked rice.

Sweet and Sour Chicken Stir-Fry

Ingredients:

- 1 lb chicken breast, cubed
- 1 bell pepper, chopped
- 1 cup pineapple chunks
- 1 onion, chopped
- 2 cloves garlic, minced
- 3 tbsp sweet and sour sauce
- 1 tbsp vegetable oil
- Cooked rice for serving

Instructions:

1. **Heat Oil:** In a large skillet or wok, heat vegetable oil over medium-high heat.
2. **Cook Chicken:** Add chicken and stir-fry for about 5-7 minutes until cooked through.
3. **Add Vegetables:** Add bell pepper, pineapple, onion, and garlic; stir-fry for an additional 3-4 minutes.
4. **Add Sauce:** Stir in sweet and sour sauce; cook for another minute.
5. **Serve:** Serve over cooked rice.

Vegetable Lo Mein Stir-Fry

Ingredients:

- 8 oz lo mein noodles
- 2 cups mixed vegetables (bell peppers, carrots, snap peas)
- 2 cloves garlic, minced
- 1 tbsp ginger, minced
- 3 tbsp soy sauce
- 1 tbsp sesame oil
- 1 tbsp vegetable oil

Instructions:

1. **Cook Noodles:** Cook lo mein noodles according to package instructions; drain and set aside.
2. **Heat Oil:** In a large skillet or wok, heat vegetable oil over medium-high heat.
3. **Add Vegetables:** Add mixed vegetables, garlic, and ginger; stir-fry for about 4-5 minutes.
4. **Combine Noodles:** Add cooked noodles and soy sauce; stir-fry for another 2-3 minutes.
5. **Serve:** Drizzle with sesame oil and serve.

Thai Basil Beef Stir-Fry

Ingredients:

- 1 lb beef flank steak, thinly sliced
- 2 cups fresh basil leaves
- 1 bell pepper, sliced
- 2 cloves garlic, minced
- 1 tbsp ginger, minced
- 3 tbsp soy sauce
- 1 tbsp oyster sauce
- 1 tbsp vegetable oil

Instructions:

1. **Heat Oil:** In a large skillet or wok, heat vegetable oil over medium-high heat.
2. **Cook Beef:** Add sliced beef and stir-fry for about 3-4 minutes until browned.
3. **Add Vegetables:** Add bell pepper, garlic, and ginger; stir-fry for an additional 2-3 minutes.
4. **Add Sauces and Basil:** Stir in soy sauce, oyster sauce, and basil; cook for another minute.
5. **Serve:** Serve over cooked rice.

Black Bean Chicken Stir-Fry

Ingredients:

- 1 lb chicken breast, sliced
- 1 cup black beans, rinsed and drained
- 1 bell pepper, chopped
- 2 cloves garlic, minced
- 3 tbsp soy sauce
- 1 tbsp vegetable oil
- Cooked rice for serving

Instructions:

1. **Heat Oil:** In a large skillet or wok, heat vegetable oil over medium-high heat.
2. **Cook Chicken:** Add sliced chicken and stir-fry for about 5-7 minutes until cooked through.
3. **Add Vegetables:** Add bell pepper and garlic; stir-fry for an additional 3-4 minutes.
4. **Add Black Beans:** Stir in black beans and soy sauce; cook for another minute.
5. **Serve:** Serve over cooked rice.

Sesame Tofu and Broccoli

Ingredients:

- 14 oz firm tofu, pressed and cubed
- 2 cups broccoli florets
- 2 cloves garlic, minced
- 3 tbsp soy sauce
- 1 tbsp sesame oil
- 1 tbsp vegetable oil
- Sesame seeds for garnish
- Cooked rice for serving

Instructions:

1. **Heat Oil:** In a large skillet or wok, heat vegetable oil over medium-high heat.
2. **Cook Tofu:** Add cubed tofu and stir-fry until golden brown, about 5-7 minutes.
3. **Add Broccoli:** Add broccoli and garlic; stir-fry for an additional 4-5 minutes until broccoli is tender.
4. **Add Sauce:** Stir in soy sauce and sesame oil; cook for another minute.
5. **Serve:** Garnish with sesame seeds and serve over cooked rice.

Orange Chicken Stir-Fry

Ingredients:

- 1 lb chicken breast, cubed
- 1 cup orange juice
- 1 bell pepper, chopped
- 2 cloves garlic, minced
- 2 tbsp soy sauce
- 1 tbsp cornstarch
- 1 tbsp vegetable oil
- Cooked rice for serving

Instructions:

1. **Marinate Chicken:** In a bowl, combine cubed chicken with orange juice and soy sauce; let marinate for 15 minutes.
2. **Heat Oil:** In a large skillet or wok, heat vegetable oil over medium-high heat.
3. **Cook Chicken:** Add marinated chicken and stir-fry for about 5-7 minutes until cooked through.
4. **Add Vegetables:** Add bell pepper and garlic; stir-fry for an additional 3-4 minutes.
5. **Thicken Sauce:** Stir in cornstarch mixed with a little water; cook until thickened.
6. **Serve:** Serve over cooked rice.

Hoisin Beef and Broccoli Stir-Fry

Ingredients:

- 1 lb beef sirloin, thinly sliced
- 2 cups broccoli florets
- 2 cloves garlic, minced
- 1 tbsp ginger, minced
- 3 tbsp hoisin sauce
- 1 tbsp soy sauce
- 1 tbsp vegetable oil
- Cooked rice for serving

Instructions:

1. **Heat Oil:** In a large skillet or wok, heat vegetable oil over medium-high heat.
2. **Cook Beef:** Add sliced beef and stir-fry for about 3-4 minutes until browned.
3. **Add Broccoli:** Add broccoli, garlic, and ginger; stir-fry for an additional 4-5 minutes.
4. **Add Sauces:** Stir in hoisin sauce and soy sauce; cook for another minute.
5. **Serve:** Serve over cooked rice.

Enjoy your delicious stir-fry meals!

Kung Pao Chicken Stir-Fry

Ingredients:

- 1 lb chicken breast, diced
- 1/2 cup peanuts
- 1 bell pepper, chopped
- 1/2 cup scallions, chopped
- 3 cloves garlic, minced
- 1 tbsp ginger, minced
- 3 tbsp soy sauce
- 1 tbsp rice vinegar
- 1 tbsp sesame oil
- 1 tsp red pepper flakes
- 1 tbsp vegetable oil

Instructions:

1. **Heat Oil:** In a large skillet or wok, heat vegetable oil over medium-high heat.
2. **Cook Chicken:** Add diced chicken and stir-fry until cooked through, about 5-7 minutes.
3. **Add Vegetables:** Add bell pepper, garlic, ginger, and scallions; stir-fry for an additional 3-4 minutes.
4. **Add Sauce:** Stir in soy sauce, rice vinegar, sesame oil, peanuts, and red pepper flakes; cook for another minute.
5. **Serve:** Serve hot over rice.

Garlic Snow Peas and Mushrooms

Ingredients:

- 2 cups snow peas, trimmed
- 1 cup mushrooms, sliced
- 3 cloves garlic, minced
- 1 tbsp vegetable oil
- 1 tbsp soy sauce
- Sesame seeds for garnish

Instructions:

1. **Heat Oil:** In a skillet, heat vegetable oil over medium-high heat.
2. **Cook Mushrooms:** Add mushrooms and sauté for 2-3 minutes until soft.
3. **Add Snow Peas:** Add snow peas and garlic; stir-fry for an additional 3-4 minutes.
4. **Add Sauce:** Stir in soy sauce and cook for another minute.
5. **Serve:** Garnish with sesame seeds and serve hot.

Spicy Pork and Bok Choy Stir-Fry

Ingredients:

- 1 lb pork tenderloin, thinly sliced
- 2 cups bok choy, chopped
- 2 cloves garlic, minced
- 1 tbsp ginger, minced
- 3 tbsp soy sauce
- 1 tbsp chili paste
- 1 tbsp vegetable oil

Instructions:

1. **Heat Oil:** In a large skillet or wok, heat vegetable oil over medium-high heat.
2. **Cook Pork:** Add sliced pork and stir-fry for about 5-7 minutes until browned.
3. **Add Vegetables:** Add bok choy, garlic, and ginger; stir-fry for another 3-4 minutes.
4. **Add Sauce:** Stir in soy sauce and chili paste; cook for another minute.
5. **Serve:** Serve hot over rice or noodles.

Sweet Chili Shrimp and Veggies

Ingredients:

- 1 lb shrimp, peeled and deveined
- 2 cups mixed vegetables (bell peppers, broccoli, carrots)
- 3 tbsp sweet chili sauce
- 3 cloves garlic, minced
- 1 tbsp vegetable oil

Instructions:

1. **Heat Oil:** In a large skillet or wok, heat vegetable oil over medium-high heat.
2. **Cook Shrimp:** Add shrimp and cook for 2-3 minutes until pink and cooked through.
3. **Add Vegetables:** Add mixed vegetables and garlic; stir-fry for an additional 4-5 minutes.
4. **Add Sauce:** Stir in sweet chili sauce; cook for another minute.
5. **Serve:** Serve over rice or noodles.

Lemon Garlic Chicken Stir-Fry

Ingredients:

- 1 lb chicken breast, sliced
- 2 cups broccoli florets
- 3 cloves garlic, minced
- 1 lemon, juiced and zested
- 3 tbsp soy sauce
- 1 tbsp vegetable oil

Instructions:

1. **Heat Oil:** In a large skillet or wok, heat vegetable oil over medium-high heat.
2. **Cook Chicken:** Add sliced chicken and stir-fry until cooked through, about 5-7 minutes.
3. **Add Broccoli:** Add broccoli and garlic; stir-fry for another 3-4 minutes.
4. **Add Sauce:** Stir in lemon juice, zest, and soy sauce; cook for another minute.
5. **Serve:** Serve hot over rice.

Pad Thai Vegetable Stir-Fry

Ingredients:

- 8 oz rice noodles
- 2 cups mixed vegetables (carrots, bell peppers, bean sprouts)
- 2 eggs, beaten
- 3 tbsp pad thai sauce
- 3 cloves garlic, minced
- 1 tbsp vegetable oil
- Lime wedges for serving

Instructions:

1. **Cook Noodles:** Cook rice noodles according to package instructions; drain and set aside.
2. **Heat Oil:** In a large skillet or wok, heat vegetable oil over medium-high heat.
3. **Cook Eggs:** Add beaten eggs and scramble until cooked; remove from pan.
4. **Add Vegetables:** Add mixed vegetables and garlic; stir-fry for about 4-5 minutes.
5. **Combine Ingredients:** Add cooked noodles, eggs, and pad thai sauce; toss to combine and heat through.
6. **Serve:** Serve hot with lime wedges.

Korean Beef Bulgogi Stir-Fry

Ingredients:

- 1 lb beef sirloin, thinly sliced
- 1 onion, sliced
- 1 carrot, julienned
- 3 tbsp bulgogi sauce
- 1 tbsp sesame oil
- 1 tbsp vegetable oil
- Cooked rice for serving

Instructions:

1. **Heat Oil:** In a large skillet or wok, heat vegetable oil over medium-high heat.
2. **Cook Beef:** Add sliced beef and stir-fry for about 3-4 minutes until browned.
3. **Add Vegetables:** Add onion and carrot; stir-fry for another 3-4 minutes.
4. **Add Sauce:** Stir in bulgogi sauce and sesame oil; cook for another minute.
5. **Serve:** Serve hot over rice.

Teriyaki Tofu and Vegetable Stir-Fry

Ingredients:

- 14 oz firm tofu, pressed and cubed
- 2 cups mixed vegetables (bell peppers, broccoli, carrots)
- 3 tbsp teriyaki sauce
- 3 cloves garlic, minced
- 1 tbsp vegetable oil
- Sesame seeds for garnish

Instructions:

1. **Heat Oil:** In a large skillet or wok, heat vegetable oil over medium-high heat.
2. **Cook Tofu:** Add cubed tofu and stir-fry until golden brown, about 5-7 minutes.
3. **Add Vegetables:** Add mixed vegetables and garlic; stir-fry for an additional 4-5 minutes.
4. **Add Sauce:** Stir in teriyaki sauce; cook for another minute.
5. **Serve:** Garnish with sesame seeds and serve hot over rice.

Enjoy these flavorful stir-fry dishes!

Thai Red Curry Chicken Stir-Fry

Ingredients:

- 1 lb chicken breast, sliced
- 1 can (14 oz) coconut milk
- 2 tbsp red curry paste
- 2 cups mixed bell peppers, sliced
- 1 cup snap peas
- 3 cloves garlic, minced
- 1 tbsp vegetable oil
- Fresh basil for garnish

Instructions:

1. **Heat Oil:** In a large skillet or wok, heat vegetable oil over medium-high heat.
2. **Cook Chicken:** Add sliced chicken and stir-fry until cooked through, about 5-7 minutes.
3. **Add Vegetables:** Add bell peppers, snap peas, and garlic; stir-fry for another 3-4 minutes.
4. **Add Sauce:** Stir in coconut milk and red curry paste; cook until heated through.
5. **Serve:** Garnish with fresh basil and serve hot over rice.

Szechuan Eggplant Stir-Fry

Ingredients:

- 1 lb eggplant, sliced
- 1 bell pepper, chopped
- 3 cloves garlic, minced
- 2 tbsp Szechuan sauce
- 1 tbsp soy sauce
- 1 tbsp vegetable oil
- Green onions for garnish

Instructions:

1. **Heat Oil:** In a large skillet or wok, heat vegetable oil over medium-high heat.
2. **Cook Eggplant:** Add eggplant and cook for about 5-7 minutes until softened.
3. **Add Vegetables:** Add bell pepper and garlic; stir-fry for another 3-4 minutes.
4. **Add Sauce:** Stir in Szechuan sauce and soy sauce; cook for another minute.
5. **Serve:** Garnish with green onions and serve hot over rice.

Honey Garlic Chicken and Broccoli

Ingredients:

- 1 lb chicken breast, sliced
- 2 cups broccoli florets
- 3 cloves garlic, minced
- 3 tbsp honey
- 3 tbsp soy sauce
- 1 tbsp vegetable oil

Instructions:

1. **Heat Oil:** In a large skillet or wok, heat vegetable oil over medium-high heat.
2. **Cook Chicken:** Add sliced chicken and stir-fry until cooked through, about 5-7 minutes.
3. **Add Broccoli:** Add broccoli and garlic; stir-fry for another 3-4 minutes until broccoli is tender.
4. **Add Sauce:** Stir in honey and soy sauce; cook for another minute.
5. **Serve:** Serve hot over rice.

Pineapple Chicken Stir-Fry

Ingredients:

- 1 lb chicken breast, diced
- 1 cup pineapple chunks
- 1 bell pepper, sliced
- 1/2 cup red onion, sliced
- 3 cloves garlic, minced
- 2 tbsp soy sauce
- 1 tbsp vegetable oil

Instructions:

1. **Heat Oil:** In a large skillet or wok, heat vegetable oil over medium-high heat.
2. **Cook Chicken:** Add diced chicken and stir-fry until cooked through, about 5-7 minutes.
3. **Add Vegetables:** Add pineapple, bell pepper, red onion, and garlic; stir-fry for another 3-4 minutes.
4. **Add Sauce:** Stir in soy sauce and cook for another minute.
5. **Serve:** Serve hot over rice.

Vegetable Fried Rice Stir-Fry

Ingredients:

- 4 cups cooked rice (preferably day-old)
- 2 cups mixed vegetables (carrots, peas, corn)
- 3 cloves garlic, minced
- 2 eggs, beaten
- 3 tbsp soy sauce
- 1 tbsp vegetable oil
- Green onions for garnish

Instructions:

1. **Heat Oil:** In a large skillet or wok, heat vegetable oil over medium-high heat.
2. **Cook Eggs:** Add beaten eggs and scramble until cooked; remove from the pan.
3. **Add Vegetables:** Add mixed vegetables and garlic; stir-fry for about 3-4 minutes.
4. **Add Rice:** Add cooked rice and soy sauce; mix well and cook for another 2-3 minutes.
5. **Combine Ingredients:** Stir in scrambled eggs and garnish with green onions; serve hot.

Five-Spice Chicken and Vegetable Stir-Fry

Ingredients:

- 1 lb chicken breast, sliced
- 2 cups mixed vegetables (bell peppers, broccoli, snap peas)
- 3 cloves garlic, minced
- 1 tbsp Chinese five-spice powder
- 3 tbsp soy sauce
- 1 tbsp vegetable oil

Instructions:

1. **Heat Oil:** In a large skillet or wok, heat vegetable oil over medium-high heat.
2. **Cook Chicken:** Add sliced chicken and stir-fry until cooked through, about 5-7 minutes.
3. **Add Vegetables:** Add mixed vegetables and garlic; stir-fry for another 3-4 minutes.
4. **Add Spice:** Stir in five-spice powder and soy sauce; cook for another minute.
5. **Serve:** Serve hot over rice.

Cashew Shrimp Stir-Fry

Ingredients:

- 1 lb shrimp, peeled and deveined
- 1 cup cashews
- 2 cups mixed vegetables (bell peppers, broccoli, carrots)
- 3 cloves garlic, minced
- 3 tbsp soy sauce
- 1 tbsp vegetable oil

Instructions:

1. **Heat Oil:** In a large skillet or wok, heat vegetable oil over medium-high heat.
2. **Cook Shrimp:** Add shrimp and stir-fry for 2-3 minutes until pink and cooked through.
3. **Add Vegetables:** Add mixed vegetables and garlic; stir-fry for another 4-5 minutes.
4. **Add Cashews and Sauce:** Stir in cashews and soy sauce; cook for another minute.
5. **Serve:** Serve hot over rice.

Spicy Garlic Tofu and Bell Peppers

Ingredients:

- 14 oz firm tofu, pressed and cubed
- 2 bell peppers, sliced
- 3 cloves garlic, minced
- 2 tbsp sriracha sauce
- 3 tbsp soy sauce
- 1 tbsp vegetable oil

Instructions:

1. **Heat Oil:** In a large skillet or wok, heat vegetable oil over medium-high heat.
2. **Cook Tofu:** Add cubed tofu and stir-fry until golden brown, about 5-7 minutes.
3. **Add Vegetables:** Add bell peppers and garlic; stir-fry for an additional 4-5 minutes.
4. **Add Sauce:** Stir in sriracha sauce and soy sauce; cook for another minute.
5. **Serve:** Serve hot over rice or noodles.

Enjoy these delicious stir-fry recipes!

Cilantro Lime Chicken Stir-Fry

Ingredients:

- 1 lb chicken breast, sliced
- 2 cups bell peppers, sliced
- 1 cup onion, sliced
- 3 cloves garlic, minced
- Juice of 2 limes
- 1/4 cup fresh cilantro, chopped
- 1 tbsp vegetable oil
- Salt and pepper to taste

Instructions:

1. **Heat Oil:** In a large skillet or wok, heat vegetable oil over medium-high heat.
2. **Cook Chicken:** Add sliced chicken and stir-fry until cooked through, about 5-7 minutes.
3. **Add Vegetables:** Add bell peppers, onion, and garlic; stir-fry for another 3-4 minutes.
4. **Add Lime and Cilantro:** Stir in lime juice, cilantro, salt, and pepper; cook for another minute.
5. **Serve:** Serve hot over rice or tortillas.

Sweet and Sour Tofu Stir-Fry

Ingredients:

- 14 oz firm tofu, pressed and cubed
- 1 cup pineapple chunks
- 1 cup bell peppers, sliced
- 1/2 cup onion, sliced
- 3 cloves garlic, minced
- 1/4 cup sweet and sour sauce
- 1 tbsp vegetable oil

Instructions:

1. **Heat Oil:** In a large skillet or wok, heat vegetable oil over medium-high heat.
2. **Cook Tofu:** Add cubed tofu and stir-fry until golden brown, about 5-7 minutes.
3. **Add Vegetables:** Add pineapple, bell peppers, onion, and garlic; stir-fry for another 4-5 minutes.
4. **Add Sauce:** Stir in sweet and sour sauce; cook for another minute.
5. **Serve:** Serve hot over rice.

Spicy Asian Pork Stir-Fry

Ingredients:

- 1 lb pork tenderloin, sliced
- 2 cups broccoli florets
- 1 cup bell peppers, sliced
- 3 cloves garlic, minced
- 2 tbsp sriracha sauce
- 3 tbsp soy sauce
- 1 tbsp vegetable oil

Instructions:

1. **Heat Oil:** In a large skillet or wok, heat vegetable oil over medium-high heat.
2. **Cook Pork:** Add sliced pork and stir-fry until cooked through, about 5-7 minutes.
3. **Add Vegetables:** Add broccoli, bell peppers, and garlic; stir-fry for another 4-5 minutes.
4. **Add Sauce:** Stir in sriracha sauce and soy sauce; cook for another minute.
5. **Serve:** Serve hot over rice or noodles.

Lemon Grass Chicken Stir-Fry

Ingredients:

- 1 lb chicken breast, sliced
- 1 cup bell peppers, sliced
- 1/2 cup onion, sliced
- 3 stalks lemongrass, minced
- 3 cloves garlic, minced
- 2 tbsp soy sauce
- 1 tbsp vegetable oil

Instructions:

1. **Heat Oil:** In a large skillet or wok, heat vegetable oil over medium-high heat.
2. **Cook Chicken:** Add sliced chicken and stir-fry until cooked through, about 5-7 minutes.
3. **Add Vegetables:** Add bell peppers, onion, lemongrass, and garlic; stir-fry for another 4-5 minutes.
4. **Add Sauce:** Stir in soy sauce; cook for another minute.
5. **Serve:** Serve hot over rice.

Thai Peanut Chicken Stir-Fry

Ingredients:

- 1 lb chicken breast, sliced
- 1 cup bell peppers, sliced
- 1 cup snap peas
- 3 cloves garlic, minced
- 1/4 cup peanut sauce
- 1 tbsp vegetable oil
- Chopped peanuts for garnish

Instructions:

1. **Heat Oil:** In a large skillet or wok, heat vegetable oil over medium-high heat.
2. **Cook Chicken:** Add sliced chicken and stir-fry until cooked through, about 5-7 minutes.
3. **Add Vegetables:** Add bell peppers, snap peas, and garlic; stir-fry for another 4-5 minutes.
4. **Add Sauce:** Stir in peanut sauce; cook for another minute.
5. **Serve:** Garnish with chopped peanuts and serve hot over rice.

Teriyaki Beef and Vegetable Stir-Fry

Ingredients:

- 1 lb beef sirloin, sliced
- 2 cups mixed vegetables (broccoli, bell peppers, carrots)
- 3 cloves garlic, minced
- 1/4 cup teriyaki sauce
- 1 tbsp vegetable oil

Instructions:

1. **Heat Oil:** In a large skillet or wok, heat vegetable oil over medium-high heat.
2. **Cook Beef:** Add sliced beef and stir-fry until cooked through, about 5-7 minutes.
3. **Add Vegetables:** Add mixed vegetables and garlic; stir-fry for another 4-5 minutes.
4. **Add Sauce:** Stir in teriyaki sauce; cook for another minute.
5. **Serve:** Serve hot over rice or noodles.

Garlic Shrimp and Zucchini Stir-Fry

Ingredients:

- 1 lb shrimp, peeled and deveined
- 2 cups zucchini, sliced
- 3 cloves garlic, minced
- 1 tbsp soy sauce
- 1 tbsp vegetable oil
- Lemon wedges for garnish

Instructions:

1. **Heat Oil:** In a large skillet or wok, heat vegetable oil over medium-high heat.
2. **Cook Shrimp:** Add shrimp and stir-fry until pink and cooked through, about 2-3 minutes.
3. **Add Zucchini:** Add zucchini and garlic; stir-fry for another 3-4 minutes.
4. **Add Sauce:** Stir in soy sauce; cook for another minute.
5. **Serve:** Garnish with lemon wedges and serve hot over rice.

Broccoli and Beef Stir-Fry with Oyster Sauce

Ingredients:

- 1 lb beef flank steak, sliced
- 2 cups broccoli florets
- 3 cloves garlic, minced
- 1/4 cup oyster sauce
- 1 tbsp vegetable oil

Instructions:

1. **Heat Oil:** In a large skillet or wok, heat vegetable oil over medium-high heat.
2. **Cook Beef:** Add sliced beef and stir-fry until cooked through, about 5-7 minutes.
3. **Add Broccoli:** Add broccoli and garlic; stir-fry for another 4-5 minutes.
4. **Add Sauce:** Stir in oyster sauce; cook for another minute.
5. **Serve:** Serve hot over rice or noodles.

Enjoy these delicious stir-fry recipes!

Miso Glazed Eggplant Stir-Fry

Ingredients:

- 2 medium eggplants, sliced
- 1 cup bell peppers, sliced
- 1/2 cup onion, sliced
- 3 cloves garlic, minced
- 1/4 cup miso paste
- 2 tbsp soy sauce
- 1 tbsp vegetable oil
- Sesame seeds for garnish

Instructions:

1. **Heat Oil:** In a large skillet or wok, heat vegetable oil over medium-high heat.
2. **Cook Eggplant:** Add sliced eggplant and stir-fry until tender, about 5-7 minutes.
3. **Add Vegetables:** Add bell peppers, onion, and garlic; stir-fry for another 3-4 minutes.
4. **Add Miso:** In a bowl, mix miso paste and soy sauce, then stir into the vegetable mixture; cook for another 2 minutes.
5. **Serve:** Garnish with sesame seeds and serve hot over rice.

Spicy Szechuan Chicken and Noodles

Ingredients:

- 1 lb chicken breast, sliced
- 8 oz noodles (such as rice noodles or egg noodles)
- 2 cups mixed vegetables (broccoli, carrots, bell peppers)
- 3 cloves garlic, minced
- 2 tbsp Szechuan sauce
- 1 tbsp vegetable oil
- Green onions for garnish

Instructions:

1. **Cook Noodles:** Cook noodles according to package instructions, then drain and set aside.
2. **Heat Oil:** In a large skillet or wok, heat vegetable oil over medium-high heat.
3. **Cook Chicken:** Add sliced chicken and stir-fry until cooked through, about 5-7 minutes.
4. **Add Vegetables:** Add mixed vegetables and garlic; stir-fry for another 4-5 minutes.
5. **Combine:** Stir in cooked noodles and Szechuan sauce; toss to combine.
6. **Serve:** Garnish with green onions and serve hot.

Sesame Ginger Shrimp Stir-Fry

Ingredients:

- 1 lb shrimp, peeled and deveined
- 2 cups snap peas
- 1 cup bell peppers, sliced
- 3 cloves garlic, minced
- 1 tbsp ginger, minced
- 3 tbsp soy sauce
- 1 tbsp sesame oil
- Sesame seeds for garnish

Instructions:

1. **Heat Oil:** In a large skillet or wok, heat sesame oil over medium-high heat.
2. **Cook Shrimp:** Add shrimp and stir-fry until pink and cooked through, about 2-3 minutes.
3. **Add Vegetables:** Add snap peas, bell peppers, garlic, and ginger; stir-fry for another 3-4 minutes.
4. **Add Sauce:** Stir in soy sauce; cook for another minute.
5. **Serve:** Garnish with sesame seeds and serve hot over rice.

Thai Coconut Chicken Stir-Fry

Ingredients:

- 1 lb chicken breast, sliced
- 1 cup bell peppers, sliced
- 1 cup zucchini, sliced
- 3 cloves garlic, minced
- 1 can (14 oz) coconut milk
- 2 tbsp Thai curry paste
- 1 tbsp vegetable oil

Instructions:

1. **Heat Oil:** In a large skillet or wok, heat vegetable oil over medium-high heat.
2. **Cook Chicken:** Add sliced chicken and stir-fry until cooked through, about 5-7 minutes.
3. **Add Vegetables:** Add bell peppers, zucchini, and garlic; stir-fry for another 3-4 minutes.
4. **Add Coconut Milk:** Stir in coconut milk and Thai curry paste; cook for another 2-3 minutes until heated through.
5. **Serve:** Serve hot over rice or noodles.

Lemon Ginger Tofu Stir-Fry

Ingredients:

- 14 oz firm tofu, pressed and cubed
- 2 cups broccoli florets
- 1 cup bell peppers, sliced
- 3 cloves garlic, minced
- 1 tbsp ginger, minced
- Juice of 1 lemon
- 2 tbsp soy sauce
- 1 tbsp vegetable oil

Instructions:

1. **Heat Oil:** In a large skillet or wok, heat vegetable oil over medium-high heat.
2. **Cook Tofu:** Add cubed tofu and stir-fry until golden brown, about 5-7 minutes.
3. **Add Vegetables:** Add broccoli, bell peppers, garlic, and ginger; stir-fry for another 4-5 minutes.
4. **Add Lemon and Sauce:** Stir in lemon juice and soy sauce; cook for another minute.
5. **Serve:** Serve hot over rice or quinoa.

Egg Foo Young Stir-Fry

Ingredients:

- 4 eggs, beaten
- 1 cup bean sprouts
- 1 cup cabbage, shredded
- 1/2 cup carrots, shredded
- 3 green onions, sliced
- 2 tbsp soy sauce
- 1 tbsp vegetable oil

Instructions:

1. **Heat Oil:** In a large skillet, heat vegetable oil over medium heat.
2. **Make Omelets:** Pour in beaten eggs to form a round omelet; add bean sprouts, cabbage, carrots, and green onions on top.
3. **Cook:** Cook until set, about 3-4 minutes per side; flip carefully.
4. **Serve:** Serve hot with soy sauce drizzled on top.

Curry Vegetable Stir-Fry

Ingredients:

- 2 cups mixed vegetables (broccoli, bell peppers, carrots)
- 1 cup cauliflower florets
- 3 cloves garlic, minced
- 2 tbsp curry powder
- 1 can (14 oz) coconut milk
- 1 tbsp vegetable oil

Instructions:

1. **Heat Oil:** In a large skillet or wok, heat vegetable oil over medium-high heat.
2. **Add Garlic and Vegetables:** Add garlic and mixed vegetables; stir-fry for about 4-5 minutes.
3. **Add Curry Powder:** Stir in curry powder; cook for another minute.
4. **Add Coconut Milk:** Pour in coconut milk; bring to a simmer and cook for an additional 5 minutes.
5. **Serve:** Serve hot over rice or quinoa.

Enjoy these delicious stir-fry recipes!

Stir-Fried Udon Noodles with Veggies

Ingredients:

- 12 oz udon noodles
- 2 cups mixed vegetables (carrots, bell peppers, broccoli)
- 3 cloves garlic, minced
- 2 tbsp soy sauce
- 1 tbsp sesame oil
- 1 tbsp vegetable oil
- Green onions for garnish

Instructions:

1. **Cook Udon Noodles:** Cook udon noodles according to package instructions, drain, and set aside.
2. **Heat Oil:** In a large skillet or wok, heat vegetable oil over medium-high heat.
3. **Stir-Fry Vegetables:** Add minced garlic and mixed vegetables; stir-fry for about 4-5 minutes until vegetables are tender.
4. **Add Noodles and Sauce:** Add cooked udon noodles and soy sauce; toss to combine and heat through for about 2-3 minutes.
5. **Serve:** Drizzle with sesame oil, garnish with green onions, and serve hot.

Honey Soy Chicken and Veggie Stir-Fry

Ingredients:

- 1 lb chicken breast, sliced
- 2 cups mixed vegetables (snap peas, bell peppers, carrots)
- 3 cloves garlic, minced
- 1/4 cup honey
- 2 tbsp soy sauce
- 1 tbsp vegetable oil

Instructions:

1. **Heat Oil:** In a large skillet or wok, heat vegetable oil over medium-high heat.
2. **Cook Chicken:** Add sliced chicken and stir-fry until cooked through, about 5-7 minutes.
3. **Add Garlic and Vegetables:** Add garlic and mixed vegetables; stir-fry for another 3-4 minutes.
4. **Add Sauce:** Stir in honey and soy sauce; cook for another 2 minutes, coating everything well.
5. **Serve:** Serve hot over rice or noodles.

Teriyaki Vegetable and Tofu Stir-Fry

Ingredients:

- 14 oz firm tofu, pressed and cubed
- 2 cups mixed vegetables (broccoli, bell peppers, carrots)
- 3 cloves garlic, minced
- 1/4 cup teriyaki sauce
- 1 tbsp vegetable oil
- Sesame seeds for garnish

Instructions:

1. **Heat Oil:** In a large skillet or wok, heat vegetable oil over medium-high heat.
2. **Cook Tofu:** Add cubed tofu and stir-fry until golden brown, about 5-7 minutes.
3. **Add Garlic and Vegetables:** Add garlic and mixed vegetables; stir-fry for another 4-5 minutes.
4. **Add Teriyaki Sauce:** Pour in teriyaki sauce; cook for another 2-3 minutes until heated through.
5. **Serve:** Garnish with sesame seeds and serve hot over rice or noodles.

Enjoy these delicious stir-fry recipes!